Creativity
is a
null and void
contract
when it
becomes common.

THE MACABRE ERUDITE

QHUXION

the world will not make space for you-
you already take up space in its existence;
it is all been equipped with the facilities and wherewithal
to house and withstand the complexities
you've been destined and burdened with.
So reclaim the vastness of your identity
leased and loaned out to lecherous licentious immoral leeches
sucking the life, hope and love out of you
because you time after time doubted
if the world was ready or could handle all the idiosyncrasies
you are so brilliantly plagued with.
Show the world what you've ceaselessly shown yourself.
Know that you did it, take stock in the fact that you did it
and the world will know what you've always known-
that you more than just belong....
you are divinely created to manifest
the entirety of your entirety wholly and entirely.

First paperback edition August 2021
Foto Taken by MassCreatvty
978-0-578-96329-7
Published by Grammerlin Square
www.grammerlinsquare.com
grammerlinsq@gmail.com

QUIRKPOSE

the following projects are not meant to be
your ordinarily written projects;
I do not care for the rules of the status quo
or any other failings that their normalcies dictate.
will continue to creatively do as I please pursuant to the ordinances
of the Qhubiverse found on page 555 paragraph 8,
the 13th sentence in the Meridinisian Section
of the Alqhumetrical Constitution
written by the First Fifthian in the Aurum Magnus Liber.
This book was constructed to dance within the bondage
of a truer more honest freedom that caters to the soul of the writer
and not the applause of lesser beings incapable of appreciating
what they themselves can not create.

Welcome to the Qhubiverse.

Greatness Inkarcerated

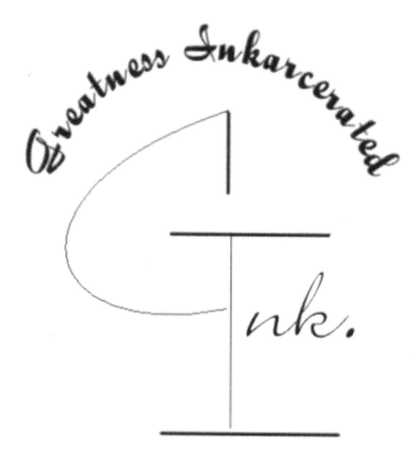

nk.

Greatness Is No Honour

THE MACABRE ERUDITE

PRESENTS:

VAGRANT GRANDILOQUENCE

Injongo:

This project recalls the creativity of my youth,
it pays homage to the journey of how and who I came to be.
I think far too often we praise the harvest
without giving too much credence
or appreciating every step of the journey,
let alone every tear and moment of excitement;
how soon we forget the circumstances of doubt
and the occasional bouts of insecurities.
This is my standing ovation for a chapter in my life
that I let go hidden and unannounced;
far too many times I talked me out of loving myself
and cheated the world out of my brilliance, no longer.

No longer will I overthink
the responses or reception of my gifts and talents;
no longer will I use the possibility of failure
to rule over my mind and my efforts,
nor will I allow fear of the small things
to Voltron their way into the path of my giftings.
For far too long and too many times to count,
I'd settled for anonymity and quiet whispers of my talent,
wanting to showcase my version
of brilliance and I kept muting myself for no good reason-
no longer.

No longer will psych myself up to purport fake
my dopeness into unrealised misery.
No longer will I sabotage my progress
for sake of whatever excuse I can muster up while clamouring for more
but simmering inside the shallow pool of mental assent.
I choose to do better by myself for myself, I choose to honour the sacrifices
I undertook naively to build a better world for the little boy
in me that grew up painfully too early
and the man in me that learned what it meant to be one too late.
This Vagrant Grandiloquence is my youthful arrogance on display
coming out of the most tumultuous time in my life.

Welcome, please enjoy what I endured.

BOCA ŠARMA

(I wish for) A Beautiful Death
(in this) Stadium of Disdain (therefore, I must say)
Auf Wiedersehen Mi Amado Inmortal.
This Collaboration With Pain (made me)
Susceptible to Failure.
(I've come to) Terms (with this)
Subconscious Excavation.
(I tried desperately) Cheating History (with the)
Escape (since) Lurelie (gave) Jaqh
Deepthroat (with) The Mask (on)
(in the) Sea of Forgetfulness
(while the) Patronus Charm (watches, repulsed)
(trying to) Switch Channels (singing)
Canon Music

Foretaste:

"I wish to devour as much as I can
for it brings me great peace and relaxation;
whether stabbing in anger or with patience,
granting them a breathless performance
while they experience the breath-taking joy
of asphyxiation..."

Collaboration with Pain

Finally, we meet. It's about time we had a face to face.
How does one who is physical and one that's abstract greet?

Agreement:
You bare a smile and I will for a day receive disdain without cease.

Was I some lucky winner or was it hereditary?
For the pain sticks out like the back of a dromedary
Seems like forever that I've been in your ward
Locked up every day like a criminal in solitary
Why did you choose to father me?
I was never able to swim
Life was the sea but I travelled in your agonizing ferry.

What did I do to fault you or gain your attention?
Why have you declined my progression?
What chapter did I miss in your generous giving of lessons?
Did I walk through without getting your permission?
Was I supposed to pay before assuming free admission?
Was I supposed to be successful with no restriction?

Why do you stick to me like needles in the skin?
My life was a wrestling match
I lost even though I never got pinned nor did I ever submit.
I must be the job that you failed to quit.
You have had my tears, my blood now you attack my spit
In a cold house trying to reach out to the world
While in my mental solarium I uneasily sit.

Will you leave if I slit my wrist?
Would you if I gave heaven a goodbye kiss?
Or will you antagonize my spirit because you fail to desist?
What is it that has made you take some sort of favour towards me?
Because I am starting to doubt the love from my Jehovah Jireh.

More and more I see the scars on my soul
And conclude why will anyone love me.

Unchain my life from your presence so I can live freely
Why won't you just get the hell away from me!!!

Eradicate yourself from my present and future being,
All I am enticed with is pain
because you are blocking my scene
You're all I'm seeing
Mount Painmore is where I'm skiing,
Down into a river or lake that is superior
Where I'm led to swim in a battle's creek
Where demons help me not
Their joy they liberally excrete.
As I paddle backward to meet my dam
Pain why have chosen to petrify Adam?

Pain:
I've existed as long as I can
I roam the earth because I cannot stand
I torment him because
He has the courage to withstand
And he explains himself better than
The rest attempt to understand
But the real reason I torment him so
Simply because I am Pain and I can

Adehun Na (Terms)

ChL:
Do you offer terms for I offer none?

Creativity:
Peradventure we might agree,
bring about light to what you have shunned

ChL:
What have thee to offer to gain my passionate services?
What terms have you brought;
make known unto me what your purpose is
Offer me not lucre, for slavery is but a distant planet
where paradise is ne'er found
Will you grant me security where love and life surely abound?
What will be your arrangement for us to be in accord?
Is it tangible in my lifetime, or is it the bliss
which no living mortal can afford
What have you thought of in regards to your plan for me?
Will I be set free or will you swindle
and trap my ingenuity for hours beyond eternity
I have seen what you have become,
purely a skeleton to that of your glory days
Why have you chosen to seek me now?

Our union seemeth unlikely
for vanity rules the page it looks like these days
What have you to say, propose or ask?
Notwithstanding that, I trust nothing of a separate nature
For betrayal is quite easy gaining trust is the task

Creativity:
I have need for thee my friend,
lo in verity and righteousness I come
Be not wary of me, I have heard of thy counsel;
the Council of Creativity
I hold you in high regard, for my essence isn't lost with thee
I am ashamed of what they call art, moreover what they call Poetry

They maim me and lie, mould a new definition
Merely rhyme lines, attach a title
and the label "poet" is their acquisition
I hide for they seek to plunder and rape, loot and pillage
I house many lovers of my argot,
but they know of none in my village
I need you, to spread the word,
to those whom understand not what they have heard

Bring light to this madness for my existence is drifting
In oblivion sinking, what is important is not affordable,
patience is expensive

My secrets are not merely a page, my history is extensive
I need you my friend; my appetite for beauty has yet to be quenched
Bring about the right aroma while you rid my name of this filthy stench

I bring all that is attached to me, before the 21st century
All that is goodly, creativity and originality I'll share
I believe we can make a flourishing pair
I offer no money, for these things that cannot be bought are worth more
Make your league with me and change will be sure

ChL:
A flourishing pair says thee, about a union that exists not
Poetry is not the way of art anymore, the appreciation stopped
I am but one man who is ignored from day to day
Never has dark night seen the sun's bright rays?
I love who you were, but, but... you have never changed!?
It's the people who have made your person diluted and estranged.

I agree to join with thee, if your alliances come subjected to my council
For I will not leave my wits for glory yet unattained
Majesty is gaudy and my verses are unfeigned
Your foothold must be regained; your memories will be retained.
A return on your investment, great poems shall be set free
While aping shall be enslaved I agree to these terms so for as long
as I can my pen will ne'er flee the page.

SUSCEPTIBLE TO FAILURE

I bet you wake up each morning looking for Mr. Right
You're looking for the perfect guy
One whose attractive element can be seen with or without the eyes
Strong both physically and emotionally
One who keeps stroking so you can enjoy the finale
The perfect guy without embellished hoop dreams
Just a beautiful man who pushes you with love
so you can accomplish your dreams
And with each of your accomplishments achieved
he tells you he always believed
The kind of masterpiece you tell your girls
that he is everything and all you need
He is Mr. Perfect, Mr. Can't Do No Wrong,
Mr. Kiss The Right Spot, and Mr. All Night Long...

Sadly I am not him
I am far from perfect compared
to your hopes of excellence
I am probably worthless in comparison...
to your ex's maybe even to your standards
I don't have much value.
But I can give you effort
and all my intentions and words are true.
I may not be as big or as talented
Yet I can be a firm shoulder whenever you feel depressed
I may not be sexually adept
but your every ill thought I would tenderly caress.
I'd tell you every day that your love takes away my heart's rest
Because your presence continually speeds up my heart rate
I can give you sensual baths and kiss away the sweat on your face
Yearly I'd sweep you off your feet
Your voice will be the sound waves that would be on repeat
I know I work three minimum wage jobs
The house is untidy because of me sometimes
And most of my friends are unemployed slobs
But I'll cook for you and wash all the dishes
Massage you feet until the career of the pain is finished

Sometimes I'll raise my voice and behave
as though you have no choice
Occasionally I'd tell you that you suck
And I'll be cluelessly insensitive when you fall out of luck
But...but... if I get you pregnant I won't deny and I won't complain
I'd stay up all night convincing you to accept my last name
When our pride is born I'd get up to feed the kids
And take them to the park on your busy weekends

I'm not promising you Mr. Right
However I can guarantee,
you will go to bed with a smile each night
I don't do all the things you like but I'm willing to learn
Willing to love and respect your every concern
I can't promise you perfection on my part
but I can give you my word
That you'll be happier in the end
way better than it was at the start
I am a couple journeys away
from having your hopes of excellent behaviour
I know I'm not Mr. Perfect
But would you give me a chance
knowing I was susceptible to failure?

DEEP THROAT

going through it again
further and further
'til it's on my larynx
it's stuck, but it's moving
in the crevice of my mouth

stuck but moving
just in there grooving
looking at you with no words to speak
my head slowly rocking
while you try to find pleasure
in this misery

the motion of my head is unstopping
attempting my best
not to bite my tongue
finding saliva around my gum
you staring at me with squinted eyes

wondering when i will be done
disappointed by my actions
i can't wait to see the awkward aura run
it's wedged in between
the pharynx and the epiglottis

emotionally gagging
doing my best yet again not to throw up
so i hold on knowing that you need to be pleasured
therefore i cannot give up
glancing at you every now and again
as you begin to look like this is the end....

look baby... your my world and my life
never have i been the sentimental type
love is something that is rooted in the actions
but my behaviour hasn't been too whole
just movements filled with emotional fractions

I'm gagging on it on baby
trying hard to see a reason
not to commit treason
so your love can continue
after its desire to retire after this season

you now look at me intently
waiting impatiently
hurling emotional threats menacingly
"baby it's not like me to do it
whenever you want it
i honestly wish you could just keep it"
so i wouldn't have to repeat it.
why are you so adamant
if it makes me uncomfortable?
isn't it still obvious,
isn't the animation of my heart still observable?

can we release the conversation
and the negative emotions?
yes i should be pleasuring you
yes i am honest and my words are true
why am i gagging?
it's not something that i am used to
but since you need to be pleasured

I'll say it
cough, clears throat, cough

I love you.

Mi Amado Inmortal

Devoted to this splendid soul whom I love in life
For she is the underlying theme of my thoughts
The cohesion of excellence exerted in all that I inscribe
Exalted above all feminine views that exist
Better than all the beautiful women a man's fantasy consists... of
There is no light that brightens brighter than my shade of love

Dear My Immortal Beloved:
As tears flow down my eyes I blissfully reminisce
Of the days I would starve without your kiss
Your smiles torment pleasurably
while perusing through my memories

Amazing woman who has rapt me
in her enjoyable existence
Until eternity is temporary I, a blemished mortal
Will attempt to adore you unconditionally
Let those who esteem beauty
lay claim to substance in their subsistence
For old age reaches those who evade with terrorizing persistence
Beauty is but a rose that withers and fades away
But love once invoked is stationary yet progressive always

To fathom separation
Is sinfully agonizing and sabotage at best
Keeping you in my mind
is but a daydream I love to experience
Experiencing bliss at reality speed
your presence fulfils my every need
I am told never to say never so I will not, but...
At no time in this world or the next will our love cease to exist

By any means necessary
Regardless of what fate has aligned for us to rule out to
The love I have for you can never be measured or calculated
As we grow in love my ever-after let us do so in romance and laughter
Trials tested us as waves flirt with the sand
Keep thy eyes wide while we create an unbreakable chain with just our hands

Come what may and depart what will
Our unison shan't be spread apart regardless of guilt,
fault or gossip's skill
My immortal beloved if it were ever possible
that my tears could be used for healing
I'd cry rivers of miracle water only to baptise you in love
and rid you of any bad thing
Your life I cherish and perpetually I will do
For in times of peril and mystery,
just your very presence was enough to help me through

Mare Dell'Oblio

Tossing it in as if I want it to swim
Every ill and negative thing that I can remember
Out of the shallow nature that is me
Into this area of oblivion
This efficaciously forgetful sea

I remember not
with this ability of intentional amnesia
Because throwing it elsewhere
Provides for me an effective anaesthesia

This silent but roaring sea
which has accumulated all my embarrassment
My every moment of humiliation
Has saved me from utter torment
And has kept my life free from depression's association

In this sea I swim not, nor do I desire the backstroke
For with every glance back I know I will attain a loss of hope
The current of memories is a force I cannot fight
In translation, facing these memories
Is an obstacle with which I cannot cope
My whole mind is filled with partial memories
I remember well what was beneficial
But at this point my dark mind is filled with spots of white
My brain has become a mental galaxy

All the planets have been forgotten
I'm left with stars, pieces of the sun
A body of partiality I have become
So this life can become somewhat enjoyable
An expensive life I live
But discarding the pain has always been affordable

I won't remember your name, I will forget your face
I will no longer remember how we came about
The method to love you, I forgot what it takes

I forgot my pain remembered not the years
Which happiness from me refrained
In my life my arms are where you need to be
But at this point in my existence
I just want to be happy consistently
If ever you offend anything pertaining to me
Your existence will sink permanently in a forgetful sea

Patronus Charm

Life presents itself with painful visions
Etching itself inside my cognition with precision
Tormented thoughts tear the walls of my brain
Open to vulnerability, weakness feasts upon a feeble frame
All I seem to experience is brutality
But I try to stand strong for I treasure my sanity
Can I continue to withstand
Doing my best to avoid what society says is taboo for a man
Every effort I dispel falls as Lucifer did on his trip to hell

These events change me
Into what one would describe as a weaker being
A body of hurricanes and from me all good things seem to be fleeing
Somewhat like Louisiana, help is needed but no assistance is present
Memories are what I call on that I may feed on its good presence
I call on the memories that made me smile in times past
Just because I know how to make each delightful moment last
Karma reciprocates, excuse my every sin, but in good measure
Let the good deeds I exerted flood me without haste

Give my tough skin something different
from what has been the norm to taste
I call up on the memories of joy I experienced as a child
I call upon the power of peace that I may smile a while
Tranquillity brings forth inner light
Joy captivates the emotions of the soul
Memories illuminate a gloomy mind
The strength of my good memories
Is stronger than any superhero you may find
The shape of my protector has my mother's design
Saving me from the wiles of failure time after time

Blessed is that woman who cares most for me
With all I can and all that I am I will cherish her every memory
Beautiful is she, who shows more love than all
With the stored mental pictures of my Patronus Charm,
"tis not possible to fall

This life I live is accompanied by mischief as it goes along
Hopping and whistling coercing all to sing it's song
Sing a song of misery, while gathering no good company
Laying on the floor, while this bipolar entity
attempts to keep its foot on me
I remember when she came home from work
In my room, she would be in first
Quenching my love's gasping thirst
In her arms from off the ground I would gleefully burst
Like the memories, in her arms I was free from hurt
Forgive me I know Patronus indicates a male figure
But the influence and presence of my mother has been richer
So when life begins to earthquake with tremors scaling off the Richter
I call upon my memories,
For joy will always encompass about me
Whenever I summon Patronus' company

CHEATING HISTORY: UNDUIFABLE

If I Could,
I would cheat history of all hideous events
Design some international easy button
and continually press reset
I would rid the Jews mind that Hxtlxr ever existed
I would rid the world of tsunamis, floods and every wind
that ever whirled or twisted
I would rewrite history
and rid the Mexican's minds of conquistadors
Who forced upon them strange beliefs
I would cheat and rid the world of terrorist
so that all Gaia ever saw was world peace...

But if I could cheat history
I would rewind time back to Africa
And change up the route of the slave trade
That would mean my great, great grandfather wouldn't have had sex
With a black slave maid...I can go further
I would cheat and rid the Native Americans of ever
meeting the white man, so they could continue
to enjoy their existence in their homeland.
I would cheat history forever of Eve
eating the apple and sharing it with Adam
I would erase the pages and rewrite the constitution
I would cheat history
and write new conclusions for the Airmen on Tuskegee
I would cheat history and write a better script for life
So that in the 21st century I would be married to Emily
I would cheat history of ever knowing a Bush.

I could start in the early 1800's
Helping more blacks read more important books
I would switch up the sixties
So everyone could call the blacks white and the whites black
That way the Caucasoid of the present time would have had a hard time with life
I would rid the thought and need for ever creating an atom bomb
While alphabetically making L.O.V.E and U.N.I.T.Y
The greatest elements of explosion

I would cheat history of women
knowing as many hardships and heartaches as they did
And make it easier for every "good woman" when giving birth to kids
I would change the state of most homeless children and adults
So the world's economy could be driven by love and not money making cults
I would cheat history while making it suit my state at this present time
But why would I cheat history
Of all these historically unfortunate events
When all I would do is undo the historical pages of you and I

STADIUM OF DISDAIN

Pitted against each other as this supremacy
is tangible and not'ere a dream
Detestation accented with doggish hopes of humiliation
is the top priority of both teams
Different natures bearing witness to separate creeds
Upon the fuel granted by fans and opposing spectators they feed
Whether within the Stadio Olimpico or the Theatre of Dreams
The trailing side is anxious, hopeful and disrespectful as they scream
They scream and shout bawl out and cry,
too upset to normally speak
While their supporters in disappointment heckle
and with deafening quality shriek
They cause pandemonium and bruesome acts as Romulus roars
The intensity rises above the low planes where birds leisurely soar

They trail, however their passion pushes forward
as they view the debacle
'Tis as though an interview with losing
has their hopes of freedom shackled
In chains ne'er to be set free,
the caged bird that never sings
Just perches there while their captor
with no sense of gratefulness effortlessly travels
The onlookers stand there seemingly
baffled and fazed at their chosen side
And question if like them, their bloody element beats inside
The losers will,
will themselves out of this slump they believe
For pleasure is the thing that is made up of dreams
And dark chargers amplify the terrifying motion pictures
of nocturnal imaginings

The stadium of disdain holds two forces
that will eternally come to blows
Subtracting key factors whilst multiplying all woes
These passionate and ever colliding powerhouses
live head first to go toe to toe

Them which lead the way are pompous and high nosed
Their will they inculcate, force upon, "Christianize" and impose
Agitating each and every single defector, purist spectator and foe
They put on a spectacle for their disciples and friends
Ridiculing and jeering never knowing how it ends
Adding salt to every injury leaving no hope or amends
Jutting without caring they become the targets of revenge
Back and forth they continue as each share both ebb and flow
Oscillating the positions of victor and victim

Every addict hopes to embrace
winning in this abominable solarium
While their rivals settle their drugs
and remains inside their chosen columbarium
This stadium houses the good and the bad
One will outweigh the other at some point in each day
The manager chooses, elements of a fight
With short-lived winners and remembered losers
On display are excitement and disappointment,
showmanship and disrespect
Love of the game and disregard,
value for one's life and mental red cards

This arena holds no time for eloquent spats or verbose speeches
But whoever attempts to impose on or cause their hopes to fall
Will instantaneously with flung fists,
rising feet and accelerated weapons be greeted
My love and my pain, my body and my game-
the sunshine and the rain
The beauty and the ugly, the free and the detained
The remnants and the ne'er to remain
Both greet each other sneering
as that which I love and that which I hate
Fight en la Derby Della Corpo
They fight... fighting for supremacy
and total body power in my stadium of disdain.

Lure'Lie

At the helm of this short-lived quest for gold is what I seek
Through harsh winds and bipolar seas
Rummaging for success where confidence
and arrogance all have met Madame Meek
Sails up high, generous Zephyr blows and Apollo has us inspired
Our ignorance and naiveté fattened our aspirations
Our failures once again starved and suffered from cruel dehydration
The journey began and all was well, we jotted down our progression
Never did the quill go down for every living soul we declared we would tell
Out of the blue Zephyr was hushed while Boreas went on his rampage
The winds raged as we were unwillingly divorced from our beloved page
Distracted then separated nevertheless striving to hold on to
The ruins of the poetic blether we had all wished to share

The weather smashed and thrashed hoping to dissuade,
discourage and intimidate
Wanting desperately for us to repent, regress and turn back
Because our pursuit upon them they repudiate
Concentrating heavily on the task which lies ahead
I must reach my goal of completeness
so that another sense of duty might reach its end
Steering clear of rocks and leviathans
making peace treaties with Poseidon
No more for a while came any distractions

"Forgive me and excuse me a moment"...
"In the eagerness to succeed,
hidden is the humbling nature of failure"
"All that glitters isn't gold, but it is a great distraction"
"Where was I was ah yes,
Excuse the absentmindedness
'tis the inheritance of them before me"

We made our way safely through various diverting unknowns
Looming anxiously toward the end
Certainly unsure of what fate lies for we sailors around the bend
We sailed smoothly wondering what would our destiny be
Subsequently as fortune would have it,
Tyche blessed us with a radiant singing lady

Our pursuit is near complete, the end we soon will reach
And as we come into our ultimate view, she draws me to her
Her voice is enticing, alluring, captivating and sweet
Convincing my wits we will eventually end
I am lulled subconsciously into doubtful assurance

Slowly my tangible goal slips
to a far-flung dream of exiguous importance
I dreadfully row towards her, safety is evanescent
Darkness engulfs that which was
vibrant,
vivid...
incandescent

Drowning in melancholic euphony
No verve accompanies the thrill of completion
Nothing is left 'cept us leaving this surviving elegy
Lorelei the temptress and distracter of men
sang sardonic rhapsody until vessel and conductor met their end,
swan-song and doom
The once enthused pirate
on his trip to temporary glory and transitory Elysium
Detoured into carnage,
wooden wreckage and disheartening gloom
All the distractions that weren't eluded piled up one by one
So I, the restless poet left defeated
once again with another poem undone...

MASCHERA

in need of help; but still)..
i see through the mask
that i have created
(with insecure hands and damaged heart)

i hold it up for the world to see
(while my truth plays hide and seek)
i hide myself
for i am afraid to be me
(a wasteland of talent and potentiality)

ive struggled with my self-esteem
over the years
(i'm not good enough, oh god they know)
face to face with nothing but failures
caused me to cry galaxies of
unseen tears, i'm overwhelmed
(drowning in a tearful grand canyon
filled with my worst fears)

i.... am..... scared

someone told me to try god,
(so.... i ... prayed)
but he doesn't answer on weekends
and i always cry the hardest when the week ends
i need to be strengthened, but how can i be strong
when i'm so clueless about when being weak ends
(head in hands)

(to my flaws; i... am... prey)

(desperately) i long for the day
i can find my place and not be afraid
to hide the scars that form
disgusted landmarks on my face
(can surgery fix fake?)

i just wanna find the comfort and peace within
to not look at myself and feel unhappy in my own skin
(why was i made this way,
why wasnt i made like them)

the past has made me devastated
and now i'm starting to realize
the power of who i am (was) has faded
i miss me... i want to feel...
and be real in my own way
i know, you've been waiting a lifetime
but i'm afraid loved ones,
it wont be today.

so
.
.
.

please excuse my fake

AUF WIEDERSEHEN

I did love all of you, with whatever i could afford to
during my tumultuous struggle to live up to your selfish needs
and improbable standards-
I loved you lavishly, through the hellish inferno
of insecurities and past pain,
overwhelmed by your jealousy and unreasonable clinginess.
i still loved you, more as you were, not for who you could be;
i loved you no less even when all that was within me said leave.

yet still i gave you the partial parts of me with the discoloured
pieces of the broken rubix cube you created;
so fixated on ideas ill-formed and dilapidated,
that its evident that that the monster we now see in me
was only something hurt like you could have created.
the disappointment you have; well, you aided,
because i never claimed to be anything other
than what you denied to see
so the the pulsating pain you feel is not
because of me

simply because you chose,
to see what you wanted to see in me-
to be in you; while through osmosis or hypnosis
tried to transform me into what was,
what is and what always would have been
a blatant impossibility

I never meant to hurt you, but you turned
a deaf ear to the reality
and hardened your own heart as a formality.
Just to showcase the brutishly brutal brutality of your bitterness,
it changed the loving nature that was etched within me
to that of a desperate animal in the wilderness ...
I'm so far gone from myself, that i tried to be whole
and still failed after i attempted
to piece together the tattered shards of Broken's broken parts.
I'm now hopeless, as hope floats beyond the arm reach
of where arms reach; the pain reeked
as all defenses now defenceless were breached;

and forgiveness for you by me,
or for me by you looks bleak.
and though words aren't lost,
nor are they hard to find
i believe our date with truth
has reached its appointed time
and truthfully, i wish you happiness and joy
in its purest entirety
I am not saddened to say,
that you just wont find it through me-

Goodbye

CANNON MUSIC

driving home knowing
his wife is home cooking
singing his favourite song
"hey good looking".
ready to please her-
his wife after their drought of love and sex
thoughts of being second to her affair
has disappeared like the previous "dub"
behind his chest.

preparing to make up
he bought all her favourite items,
stepping out of the car he happily skips,
reminiscing- re-enacting all the little tricks
like where she liked to be kissed,
giddy with delight because he remembered
what she taught him.
fantasizing about her moans and screams
knowing that he is her only king
and the man of her dreams.
he opens the door and observes
an extra cell phone
picks it up scans the last received said
"my husband's not home".

he'd opened the front door slowly
so no one heard the doors creaking
ignorant was he to his spouse cheating.
she walked so holy, he never thought
she would leave the height of morals
and resorted to ever creeping.
he heard male sounds
praying that he was fixing something
other than her lack of pleasure;
flashes of their beginning
cut through his mental vision painfully.
his heart thumping in his mouth
hearing pleasure of two with words of love and
ecstasy coming from a foreign male in his house.

they,(one whose love was supposed to be devoted)
pleasure each other 'til the sweat on their skin is heavily coated;
making sounds that are melodiously harmonic.
their favourite music is their hearts beating,
their unbridled passion seals their faith
as they confirm a meeting with he who is irate.
distraught at the discovery
he sneaks into Scott's empty room his son about 26
goes into his secret spot and brings out last year's birthday gift.

looks up to the ceiling, trying to look to god
but cant because of the overwhelming feeling;
images clearer than crystal
taunt his cognition
as the foreign male inserts his disc
which compels her to reach soprano without question.

precise incision into her throbbing mansion
he thought to himself that their love making
was reminiscent of poetry;
they had the perfect rhythm all that was missing was a drum
and the husband provided that
with six deafening ones from his gun.

the foreigner got shot first
his wife screamed out then burst into tears;
he sang a song
"nevermind baby, I'll take away all your cares"
sarcastictically professing love.
she knew if he found out he would lose it
he shot her in the face
stood up rocked his head back and forth
because he was enjoying his cannon music.

Yon Bèl Lanmò

Buried by a barrage of creative thoughts and words
This that I speak of is a Beautiful Death.
Able to write no longer for this idyllic battle of pad and pen
Would have had me finished
with creativity done with words, ideas and breath.

Years have flown by and concepts have died
But with thorough and constant execution
I have yet to be defeated to my surprise
To end my tenure as poet, creativity has yet to oblige
Letters, words, sentences, paragraphs and punctuations
Line up for a fight with executions so deft
That excellence fails to aptly define.

Desperately a beautiful death is what I am seeking to find
For in this majestic event my purpose might come to light
Daily my struggles succumb to creativity
My ability to execute poem after poem exasperates me
Hoping to reach Elysium
Thoughts of bliss seem to emotionally
and mentally overtake me.

Will I write for the rest of my life?
For my hopes and aspirations, be that I will execute
A poem so magnificent that I can no longer muster up
the will to artfully describe
These thoughts that float suspiciously through my mind.

Confuse this not with poets who attain a creatively sterile brain
However, note this as a masterpiece done so well
That Satan becomes Lucifer before he fell
Utterly and indescribably beautiful

A poem to end all poems

A poem that speaks blatantly and subliminally
An execution marinated in absolute excellence
A poem that forces you to stare with allegiance

One that has the ability to be the Gospel
Christians feel the need to share
Because this poem typifies perfection in this,
this tainted atmosphere
I yearn for a beautiful death,
the fulfilment of my blessing
All before this masterpiece
were inadequate immature testings

I will write 'til I experience this beautiful death
I will write 'til I can no longer make letters,
words and paragraphs cohesively mesh
Excellence of execution is the key ingredient in every attempt
Nevertheless, I who write these words in lyrics, prose and poetry
Will not ever rest to write
'Til I reach the paramount of my blessing
and experience a beautiful death

Jaqch Trbosjek

Tabloid's Excerpt:
"Accompanied with noted anonymity
The stage left hints of virility and horrid indecency
Artistry with grave incredibility, had gruesome praise coming from onlookers
Who were held hostage by their curiosity.
Who is he, where did he come from?
Is he royalty, a local chap or is he a resident in the foreign vicinities?
He never seems to quit, deft execution one by one,
At times unsuspectingly another austere addition is done"

Sergeant & Coppers, Local Man and Woman Questioned:
What manner of man is this?
What vile ilk possesses he who effects such grisly business?
We must find this lad at once and give him just due
We must at all cost seek him before he decides he's through
For the heartless conspirator that possesses this one has us all doomed

Jaqch:
I plonk my all into every life subtracting execution
My despair and misfortune for a brief moment enjoy its nifty retribution
The next victim, she or he will be dissected until my capacity to massacre is seen
Marvellously horrifying are the poignant statistics I bring
Death plays its macabre concerto while in the soliloquy of misfortune misery sings

No respecter of persons am I as I carve and cut
Placing brilliance in my craft, travelling with pessimism as the Ghost of Christmas
Past
Sneakily and devilish in a reclusive stage I plot
Drawing verbal blueprints that make what's not done, well done that it may rot

I wish to devour as much as I can for it brings me great peace and relaxation
Whether stabbing in anger or with patience granting them a breathless performance
While they experience the breath-taking joy of asphyxiation
Writing my name in the history books as I document each killing
Wishing to find solace somehow in the anonymity I have created,
They believe that the knowledge I attain is troubled
Sort of, like an old unkempt building, falling to pieces, immensely dilapidated

Yet unsure of what may happen if I share my name
Will they accept me as sane or crazy,
problematic, fit for the asylum
For the off hinged and historical deaths I've placed
See I am deciding whether to leave the scene anonymous
Or emulate the character of Achilles in search of glory and fame

THE ESCAPE

(A survivor's motto or desperations creed
"Aut Inveniam Viam Aut Faciam"-
I Shall Either Find A Way Or Make One)

Yonder toward the horizon trouble is on the rise
It seems to foretell an inevitable and deservingly bitter demise
Life no longer walking in society's flippant stride
Smoke distorts the vivid vision of your "pristine" view
Fear rapt the cowardice embedded within, it is apparent in your eyes
The timer goes off, unconscious to self
Your once perfect life exploded without the sound of a bomb or boom
Deserted mind filled with senseless doctrines you never heard
Conceptualizing prescriptions you never tried
One begins to behave irrational, spontaneous and absurd
The abstract track meet of our lives, stupefied by what to do

You jump imaginary hurdles and run
extravagant marathons with lies
Looking for a safe haven where bliss begins and misery ceases
Where Karma dies and antagonists quit
Moreover, Christians actually have Halos
that don't shoot it just hovers
Regardless of what'er you do, until an entrance is made it only teases
For the pieces you make no peace with delays the time needed to recover
The easier you escape the higher the chances of you being overwhelmed reaches
The need to escape precedes the need to face
Although one can face something if a head was available
Instead of emotions running the headquarters

The nearest diversion that captivates you is plagued
"Tangere Vulnus, Tangere Vulnus (Don't Touch The Wound)
Amputating ties with the life of the problem while where goodness lives
Is plundered upon and made ready to be slaved
Whether it be desires of flesh or the longing for whatever is mind pleasing
Rushing with much urgency to the nearest asylum
While that which we escape from isn't budging or fleeting
Drinking at the bar of illogical, nonsensical, ludicrous hypotheses
Drunken with pure deceiving spirits and staggering elusiveness

The escape world is no longer a fantasy but your life appointed reality
A razed utopia transformed only fraudulently into a magnificent dystopia
The smoke doesn't clear, your vision worsened from the joy you've received
Comfortable with this method because of the high level of excellence
You've come accustomed to achieve
Duped effortlessly by the same pointless soliloquy folks refuse to hear
Like the Holy Ghost to an agnostic
You run to a solution and like the blown wind there was no evidence there
Running, searching for an escape, seeking refuge
Finding no peace whilst paranoia and insecurities bloom

You have been overtaken by what you hid from
In a drip of a moment one is rummaging for life in a deluge
Juking the inevitable, for what was, will be and has always been.
Escape is impossible if the problem lies within
So as you search for escape in a place with no exit
Denying that this description does not fit, into the knowledge of you
You stare unto a page reading catharsis able to relate in more than one way cant
you?

LAID TO REST

Before I knew I could wave wands of lead, ink and hands
I began creating under a name
and a term that seems to have been
the reason behind my apprehension
and reluctance to create.
I thought it cool and amazingly creative
to write under the name Greatness Incarcerated-
in my exuberant naïveté I thought it fine
despite the internal prodding and annoyance of the word
"incarcerated", being young and happy to lay claim
to such a title I moved on.... until today.

Today I will lay to rest any form of incarceration
(creative or otherwise)
and embrace the full range of my dopeness,
the full range of my idiosyncrasies i
n every way they show up and show out.
I am not weird and I am not normal,
we are the hybrid of the two....
weirmal because our weird is normal
and not meant to be measured against a standard t
hat is not of us (individually)
nor does it serve us (individually)

Today I lay to rest old ways that do not aid me
in my being and becoming my best, truest and most powerful self.
today I lay to rest old thoughts that hamper and burden
my present being that prevent me from being my best and highest truest self.
Today I renounce all the spells I casted in doubt, hate, anger and ignorance.
I renounce their power over myself
and anyone that may have been affected.
I am sorry, I wasn't aware of myself or my power
let alone the responsibility either came with.

Today I renounce and lay to rest thoughts of self-harm and injury.
I lay to rest the thoughts and ideas being ok with not succeeding
despite having life and breath to make every facet of success a reality.

Today I renounce and lay to rest boundaries
that felt like beautiful prisons of discomfort and mental resorts of misery.
I lay to rest every thought, action, default behaviour,
memory, response, hardwiring and every single thing I can think of
and that I may have forgotten, that can or would impede my journey,
to be the best version of the best me in every way possible.

I renounce and lay to rest
Greatness Incarcerated and Greatness Inkarcerated
and any impediments it brought about and caused
with and without my knowledge.
I reclaim and embrace my true and best self,
my highest being in its purest form.
I reclaim and embrace the best version of love,
affection and compassion for myself.
I grant myself the chances I robbed myself of a
nd or gave away because I didn't know any better.
I lay to rest what I've laid to rest.

Greatness Inkarcerated

Gi nk.

Greatness Is No Honour

$$\frac{^5\text{ChL}^8 \times (\text{R.G})^5 \times (\text{G}^4\text{M}^4\text{S}^4)^{13}}{\text{TGO}^{50} \times \text{SGH}^{50} \times \infty^{58}} = \text{Alqhumy}$$

ALQHUMY

I aim for that which no mere mortal
can physically obtain or read ,
knowing that where hands and failures
do not succeed
I will transcend every limit
with words and speech...

WELCOME TO THE
GrandMental Station

THIS TRIP
TAKES ON
THE MACABRIOUS DOLDRUMATICS OF...

THE MACABRE ERUDITE

PRESENTS:

THE GRANDIOSE GLOOM

The Council of Creativity

this entry serves as a reminder of my growth as a creative,
I've been wrestling with the thought
of actually calling myself a poet, a writer and or a storyteller.
Before I came to grips with my creative gift,
I steadily ran from the applause and any semblance of fame or notoriety.
I was so overwhelmed with the negativity of the unknowns
that my talent was what I was drowning in (the unknown).
I'm no longer in that frame of mind and I am sharing these pieces
with you so you can see where I've been mentally and experientially
as a human being who was unsure of his powers
and afraid of tapping into it fully.
I was nervous about being compared and not being good enough
despite hearing compliments that I didn't believe.
Grandiose Gloom for me is a celebratory release,
breaking the bonds of doubt and uncertainty-
accepting that I'm not where I was and I am destined
for so much greater than I could have ever imagined or believed.
This is me hugging the pain and hurt of my youth
and embracing the dopeness of my blessing realities
I not only faced adversities but overcame them countlessly;
the depression that derailed fates momentum;
the heartbreaks that saw me seek refuge in death-
I conquered and will continue conquering.
Welcome to the world of words from my pain and my mind;
I hope you embrace the darkness of your past
so you can see the paradise of your present
and the dopefullness forthcoming in your future.

This is
THE GRANDIOSE GLOOM

Ea Incipit:

FORETASTE:

I do. not. like. it. here...
not the taste that's in the air nor the chaos in my ear.
it is lonely here- is there no one there for me
empty and clanging- boredom takes over as I photoshop the misery;
I miss the boy in me, who I let down for the sake of my pain's buoyancy
wrapped in discomfort even the child in me can console...
so let me fill your soul with the misery only true love can dole.
oh the macabrery - spiritual chicanery and divine skulduggery;
I'm peeking at misery while peaking in misery then piquing miserably,
bearing burdens that don't belong to me.
but I must... for I must pick either these dastardly devilish drudgeries
or the ceremonial crematorials in cemeteries
ghoulish souls howl as though begging for my agony.
the moon bows while I bellow through the tragedy
I set the seasons of Misfortune and Calamity-
upon the solstice of Unfortunate and the Equinox of Malady
bask in the golden existence that is my savagery
oh how one revels in the revelry
how much longer will you count the ways
the world has made you fray... at the seams
hear my appeal rather than seeing my appeal
lamenting as I kneel
is there escape from this miserablous chill
im crawling still, upward still
the weight of letdown and "feltdowns"
tower over the spilling buckets of fear and regret now.
must I suffer here alone
on this godforsaken road that taxes joy as its toll
please free me from these glimmers of drudgeries...

BOCA ŠARMA

$$P^3 \times E^{13}$$
$$(N^8)^0$$
$$[(G^7)+ (D^8)]^1$$
$$(R^4 - V^5)^{10}$$
$$(N^8)^2$$
$$[(G^7)+ (D^8)]^8$$

DSTFL

$$(N^8)^4$$
$$[(G^7)+ (D^8)]^3$$
$$S^4 \div T^3 \times 2$$
$$[(G^7)+ (D^8)]^5$$
$$(H_2)^4(\sqrt{1/5} \times 5/8) + (6^6)^5$$
$$(N^8)^7$$
$$[(G^7)+ (D^8)]^6$$

ST²EIMS

$$(N^8)^8$$
$$[(T^4) \div (T^3 \times T_4)]^{14}$$

Audit of the Being

$$(N^8)^1$$

Abbysmala

$$[(G^7)+ (D^8)]^4$$

Iunior Mihi Cara Sui

$$[(G^7)+ (D^8)]^2$$
$$(N^8)^6$$

Bay Abyssmo

$$[(G^7)+ (D^8)]^7$$

Dopebaric Chamber
Entelechenesis

PRE- ENTELECHY: (UPSIGHDOWNABLE)

looks in the mirror
"am I enough?
am I even worth it,
whatever it is
am I worthy?
how do they do it?
how can I, when I am so nerdy?
how can I be so unwanted and disenchanted?

am I cool?
or still the reject from school?
can I be enough?
eventually worth anything?
what manner of misery is this?
I wish I was popular
I wish I had money
I wish everybody knew me for me
I wish I was appreciated
I wish I was loved
I wish I wasn't always so hurt and lonely.

does anybody see me?
do I even exist to you,
who think me invisible?
you, who that's reading this now?
did you answer the call or the question?

I wish I was more, for you all to see
I wish I was better for you to know
I wish I wasn't so shy
I wish, I really wish somebody loved me
I really wish somebody was there for me
I really wish somebody would hug me
tell me they loved me.

I really wish I wasn't an afterthought
I really wish I wasn't so down on myself
I really wish I wasn't so ugly
I really wish I wasn't so scared

I really wish I didn't feel pain all the time
I really wish somebody real was hearing my wish."
I really wish there was more than this.
I really wish it was easier than this wish.
I wish for the pain to die,
for the misery to die.
For all the bad things to die that I may come alive...
but am I worth it?

NON NOMEN ooo

who cares about the darkness
and its torrid insipidities?
who cares for the pain and all therewith?
who cares who hears?
No one does and no one will
no one shall, alas no one still.

so stop asking if and do,
don't stop doing and be
all that u were meant to be
legendary, dope and or splendidiary
be, for fullness sakes
be full of life despite the mistakes
just be... unapologetically you
not for likes, clickbait or views

be you despite what's been done to you
in spite who did it to you.
overcome all for that is your destiny
that is fate, that is what you control
the responses of heart mind and soul
no one cares about you more than you
even when you don't its still true
who you've been looking for has no name

the superhero-
the patronus charm
has no name
[insert yours]

GLIMMER OF DRUDGERY 01

it's lonely in here
insecurities reverberate louder than confident ignorance
this is a bad neighbourhood teeming with calamity and adversity.
it's lonely in here and I'm more alone in here
is that a glimmer
each glance towards makes it slimmer so it appears not.
the fruit of this labour isn't salubrious
more macabre or macarbrious-
a dire penchant for the glooms
even the pen chants its doom in hellish refrain-
with violence parlayed- belay the belay and away
for a way was not made - so I'm caged in silence- brewing violence...
from the finest Sansanite the world has ever seen

it is lonely here- is there no one there for me-
empty and clanging- boredom takes over as I photoshop the misery
in a quandary- on a conveyor belt of uncertainty-
pressing the button yet incapable to answer a question
I lament this existential jeopardy-
where mutes ask questions only the blind can understand-
seeing the dilemma unawares of what they hear-
handicaps shared- thinking cap smeared.

I do not like it here
but I am alone and the speech bears witness in every instance-
the awkward moves and hesitancies with not knowing what to do-
oh the macabrery - spiritual chicanery and divine skullduggery-
the walls close in, my eyes closes-
loneliness heightens and at this altitude
even guardian angels are frightened -
worried for me - that I may share the statistics
of being a self-casualty like the ones before me.
I see a light- but was that the one or was it just a shimmery glimmer,
maybe an oasis- should I run from or just face it-
the toothless fork in the road en route to desolation-

this glimmer is pure drudgery.

Non Nomen 002

preach to the anarchy
laying dormant within
awaken the insurrection
with terribly dread nothings
sweep over all goodness with dejections
victimising forlorn and unrelenting scorn
tongues speaking in black speech
from black teeth echoing in back streets.

feel the fear of worriment with the audience
of the dead whose silence is the loudest quietest thing said...
displaying macabrious gloom, salubrious tombs
the future looms and misery zooms in
with bitterness' chaoticscope
every shade of pain in Lucifer's kaleidoscope.

the reason to speak is the cause of a choke
coughing up angst then swallowing the whole roll
of rigormortis has become the highlight of this rigmarole;
peace slows and suffering comes enforcing taxes that takes its toll
feel the claustrophobia despair smothers
and anguish cuddles with..

feel the chilled wrath of destiny
karmas ill-favoured stepchild
who refuses to smile
then chides with guile
ill intentions guised a wailing surprise
just feel all that there can be
for it will be
you'll soon see the stubborn apex
of this lulling misery

an end to no omen- with non nomen.

must I suffer here and alone
tears fall like bad stock or worthless currency.
this here needs no rhyme just reason...
with the emptiness playing charades with me
playing unwinnable games with me
I'm peeking at misery while peaking
in misery then piquing miserably

must I suffer here and alone
crying for help guised as hearty laughter
these laughs give hope infectiously
inside I crumble and mope incessantly
may we forego all that forebodes
on this godforsaken road that taxes joy as its toll
I'm told to not fold by humans who can't console
nor control the woes that unfold
from the harvest reaped but never sowed.

must I suffer here again-
I hope not, let anguish simmer, please don't stir the pot-
melancholy is all I got since faith rots
and there seems no plot of rescue my worn out brain can concoct.
pray for me positively for inside me chemically
francium and cesium play chicken with the molecules in my brain
feel the disarray of disdain- imploding on the inside,
see anxiety on a steroid-
racing through space and time in the expanse of my mind.
I am not fine nor can love seem to find me
and know me in my true essence
the pinnacle plight of this blue lesson.

I'm crying still
looking and hopelessly staring through me
as I gaze mindlessly at my reflection in my window sill....

may you at least suffer happily.

THIS STAYS FULL – (DSTSTFL)

this aftertaste is wretchedness encased in bodily projectile
it serves as a reminder to continually go get mine.
this is inglorious and its presence injurious
I am fed up to say the least
inside this uninhabitable prison
where I sit crying on the keys.
I don't like it here,
I do not like how I've now settled
for the mega winnings
of this gloomy lottery that rewards fear.

confined to this chair where trauma cheers...
i do not like it here- penduluming between pride and stupidity-
the unknowns and all that scares.
brilliance and insanity- the proverbial rock and hard place
is only the intro to the concerto titled PalmFace-
I do not like how Discomfort comes forth
then comes first putting dreams
on its knees then in its purse- I do not like it.

I expect more and I am more,
lessening with every turn-
regret churns and bridges burn.
I do not like here nor do I like it there-
hither nor thither -
for it is hard and uneasy for the novice or beginner.
the internal sinner and clichéd unwinner
looking for satisfaction on the rabbit run
has become wearisome,
canst thou tell, where is some?

For I do not like it here and it seems to like me.
Who would've thought this likely?

I. do. not. like. it. here...

nor the taste that's in the air nor the chaos in my ear.
this taste is distasteful and for that this stays full
as a reminder to no longer come back here to the bitteries
and miseries of worries and insecurities that billow
into the dredgeries and sedimentaries
that have now become incendiary.

so set a blaze to these rearward ways
and the soul leeching state -
set ablaze this feeling that is uneasing and makes me queasy.
feel the rage as I encase my distaste on every page
then take centre stage and re-enact
these stains in soliloquilogical ways....
this feeling of ineptitude and misworth is distasteful,
and I promise myself to at no point
come back here so this feeling- this stays full.

Non Nomen 004

Just speak from the hills and valleys
of your being loudly and boldly.
let eternal echoes
wrestle forever into helpless surrenders...
say with all your might,
your hearts content
no prefacing, back tracking or erasing.
bellow it from the deepest deepest
either in tune or with ear piercing shrieks.
say it, scream it
cry it, know it
acknowledge it, believe it
manifest it, do it, prove it
show it, teach it

just don't die with it

it stinks and reeks- repulsive scents play doorman
as Monsieur Vomit prepares his speech.
the clockwork of the olfactory creaks.
the scent it permeates the very atmosphere
making it impossible to retreat.
I do not like it here-the dreariness is incontrovertible-
the plague irreversible and the one buoyant thing
to cling to is now submersible
send for help before I am out of breath
the reapers smiling about the abundance
he can collect from my dilapidated body
moonlighting as his greatest harvest
send help before they come for me.
(who, you may ask?)
Rescue in the form of oblivion comes for me.
therefore I do not like it here.
more afraid of these sounds I hear
a crown of fear adorns my hair- worn from wear-
wearing scared running from death out of breath
and arriving on time in Dante's lair.
come save me please, before they catch up to me -
my insides reek- joints creak and the stench of my mortality
signals the end for me;
then sparks the attention of the infantry- wretched infamy.
I do not like it here, nor do I fancy here to desire me.
wailing silently, hiding from them who violently
desire to savour the very bite of me.
what is your fixation, why hast thou chosen this location.
send help instead before the Sent accomplish their intent.
What words do I need to truly repent?
hear my appeal rather than seeing my appeal-
throw away the zeal that cramps me in fear
'til I'm lamenting as I kneel.
send help please-send hope too
send comfort and good fortune
so this glimmer of drudgery....

can get....

SENT TOO

it gets sent too, personifying a dragons wombs
where souls be entombed after being broomed
from life's room of surprising torment and ill-fated serendipity.
it gets sent too, after playing the embassy
for the holier than thou,
the mistaken misfits and them that operate wickedly.

it gets sent, without having incarnates having to be digestible.
without having miracles performed for it.
constantly robbing Peter to fraud Paul
with resurrections and light sightings.
being audited by the living
then being found unfair by the dead.
for if the dead die, shouldn't they come alive
in the same manner if the living die?

live to die and then die
to become a pointless and caseless jurisprudent-
wary that if the jury is prudent all will sort itself aright-
'til things become awry and they realise that to die is to die-
so they get sent too...

sent to the notice board of oblivion
it gets sent to, for doing what it was told
then came the stories of its morose
how zombies and anxiety have filled their decomposed-
the lies of how some have arose
from the woes of karmas indisposed...

this is it- where all becomes null-
from nothing remains that which is was at first,
then gets worst then bursts into the absence
with which its cursed for that gets sent too....
to the hell that hell gets sent to for that gets sent too-
either for judgement or sainthood

"I was doing what I was sent to, much like you,
doing what I was meant to
here you come being judgmental while going to judgment too-
for that which measures and get measured
gets sent too by the same laws which sent us two."
this is hell there is no need to be sentimental-
fan the flames as sparks of wildfires
falling to a blaze akin to tsunamic waves...
because that gets sent to where all things gets sent to...
then they get sent too...

GLIMMER OF DRUDGERY 05

They've been strategically eradicating this feeling of being sentimental
daggers of gloom pierce my mental; while anguish is delightfully
manufacturing distress as soul etched mementos.
So I've been sluggish yet still running-
into the finish line of restarts and false starts.
Gasping for air - as lungs desperately scatter for breaths policed by Regret's-
this is the masterpiece of Suffering's art;
woe stitched in a quilt of affliction bought in Sorrow's Dolour mart.
Its lonely here all while becoming homely here
waist deep in fear and I see I've fallen again in their snare,
oh how the Abysses cheer.

I am faint and waning and the drudgery's not waning nor faint;
dismissal glances as the moon dances - in the spotlight of the stars,
dazzling the eyes of all from afar.
Care free and bright so all that sees just freeze
from the aridity of astringent sunbeams.
Meanwhile in ungodly distress, boxed in desolation
it's been dismal, these cries for help decorating fright in my breath.
I do not like it here the ambience is foreboding
pride is for goading...

What do I do now? sweat clinging fearfully above my brow
ghoulish souls howl as though begging for my agony -
the moon bows while I bellow through the tragedy
the satellite plies- in its starry ballet
she flips and turns - my strength wanes
and my stomach churns while danger lurks
devilish apocalypse and I am not ready for the return.
so I count plastic petals'til they be imprisoned as ash in that Abbadon's urn
I sense their coming near, locked in to the pheromones of fear
now erratically scared and irrationally im paired
I look up and I see them there
"deep sighs of ultimomacarbrery"
they emerge

please just help me flee - this glimmer of drudgery

Hell-Hounds & Sirens

an unjust tandem, a most maniacal pair
they hound and haunt 'til one becomes scared
as they run into the deviant pretences of Help that cares.
Doggishly they trail you observing your places of comfort,
blindly leading you to where you'll run first
after the toils of life have left you dog tired and worn.

they chase and chase bringing your mind
to an induced state of haste-
running with pace being traced by fate while losing faith-
a gradual state of breakdowns and meltdowns, innumerably
the weight of letdown and "feltdowns"
tower over the spilling buckets of fear and regret now.

still the chase continues, over and over-
frosting over broad smiles and heartfelt cries
pinging at the sides like hunger in the wild...
the pursuit sustains as they waste no time
seeking for prey that prays 'til they're out of all the alphabets
from "plan a"- much closer they pry laughing at the tries
as the feast is spread and just lies- there in its efetal pose-
giving up for it knows its time has come to a close-
snickering silently knowing it fell for the wizardry of misery-
it goes away for theyve done their job and now an alarms sounds
for the Sirens to come and play.

they come and play after escaping from that bay
the Alqhumizta prayed away- these monsters find style in the guise
of whatever brings you peace at night-
offering a reprieve where for an eternity you'll breathe with ease-
a reality where beings live unimaginable free-
and the moment you believe and agree-
you'll see the light the myth Lazarus runs from perpetually- -
these beautiful monsters serenade
they soulishly persuade and spiritually sway
........you......

to step into the bay which at first had no name-
a paradise of eternal lies-
where you'll be mortified and eternalised -
a mortal falling for immortal lies-
seeing eternity with mortal eyes
never to be immortalised as he fell-
luciferociously by the lies...

they are the deluding coaxer-
flummering hoaxer and serenadious cajoler.
whispering, feeling, touching-
convincingly and most determiningly sorcerising
mesmerising and glammifying
the soon dead to hurry up
and die

so these Sirens can finally smile....

they salaciously slither as they speak,
alluding to secrets no one on earth is privy to.....
they say come and see-
the beauty the good lord witheld from thee-
come with me and see the legends that were-
be free for they are
and have been for Eternity's eternity-

how much longer will you count the ways
the world has made you fray- at the seams-
that once jubilant sunbeam-
now seethes when it breathes-

hissing away virility or muliebrity through your teeth when
people peopling their disease with ease- follow along now,
you'll see how one revels in the revelry -
rebelliously going against all the constraints El Bib proclaimed-
it was all switched- all this for you to be duped duplicitously -
distracted by the good you fail to upkeep meticulously.

come and see-
the glory that is in being free- die with me and see the truth
in its most objective potency.
see the veracity of their fallacy and the discrepancies of your malady.
you've come so far on this lonely ride
scared and contrite with nowhere to hide
you fell for the lies then trapped by trickeries of pride,
hounded by the turmoil that resides
and haunted by the pessimism reeking ingloporable
(inglorious, injurious, deplorable) havoc inside.
just close your eyes one last time
before we commence your unlazarusian goodbye....
calls for the hounds-
good..... –buye

Non Nomen 007

I value myself
more than the standards everyone
has in place for me...
I love myself
more than the guilt trippers...
I treat myself
kinder than the kindness
I treat others with...
I appreciate process of my journey
and I'm grateful
that I am aware of my being and becoming

I challenge myself
in love to learn
better ways to love myself
then perfect the art
of loving myself with myself

I tend to all hurt
I've experienced and heal them...
best I can in all aspects.

I raise the standards I've mastered
without becoming reckless and unkind
to any being on their journeys

Oh glimmer of drudgery
will the emptiness of it all beckon to me?
will it reach out for me
if I should then I'd retreat
recklessly then breathlessly
stay away, I pray.

oh glimmer of drudgery

come hither oh God
keep me safe
from the illustrious darkness
and the boisterous gloom
and the chaoticry that looms.
keep me safe from the subtleties
and creeping menial banalities
keep me safe eternally from the barbarism
for I do not want to be here
I want to be..... happy
but I do not like it still
is there escape from this miserablous chill.

I pray thee, keep me safe from the horrors
above and within playing tag
and "duck, duck, boo".
please I beseech thee, give ear to my needs
I dread this reality oh glimmer of drudgery
I desire to no longer toil
in an internal coup led by the devils troup
haranguing me that I wont regroup.

protect me from the misery
in the monotony of gluttony and wanton greed.
I desire to breathe in the first intention
of what it means to be free, not this crystalism of mud
that's been defiled religiously for centuries.

give me what was free, before free
became the bondage of free
that is earthly known universally and keep me safe there
with those that already made their pilgrimage there.
oh storm of macabrrious sorrowry
do not come for me...
oh God - fail not to keep me safe
for I do not like it here in this

glimmer of drudgery

ST²EIMS

speak to the emptiness is my soul
reverberate divine speeches in the quietness of my hollows
fill the mountainous voids in the caverns of my unknowns.

speak kindly
speak gently
speak softly
speak highly...

speak to the emptiness in my soul
that I may wade to life from the august anguish of the shallows
wake me up from this decay
that has me out of sorts and in dismay

tend to me sweetly
tend to me charitably
tend to me respectfully
tend... to me, tenderly...

speak to the emptiness in my soul
quaking in me, land-sliding in me
quaking then bringing me to my knees as I shudder timidly...

still me, calmly
steel me, calmly
speak into the emptiness
for my entirety.

speak to the emptiness in my soul
be there for the absence in my being
speak to the destitution peeking at its peak

speak to me
speak in to me
speak over me
lovingly, caringly and affectionately

fill me-make me full unlike any substance I've ever salivated for
bring me a reason to be whole, love me into the overflow
because the meter of my being has been low

speak kindly
speak gently
speak delicately

I speak to me about me, for me.

Non Nomen 008

buried or hidden
I cannot tell
found or risen for neither ring a bell
I was searching- for what, knoweth not I
but I was searching
looking low and confused on high
rummaging through nooks and niches
reaching for anything I never knew I needed.
I was looking for a way out the ways id gone
when I went away -
I was just wandering-
aimlessly but with conviction that id find it- (pray I find it)

whatever it is...

so I was scouring through hardships and misfortune
to find any piece of peace that was meant for me
whether heredity or divinity
but got lost thru some semblance of distortion.
tossing caution 'til hands are outstretched
grasping for something knowing nothing
but feeling everything simultaneously
smelling fear and tasting dirt
it's nonsensical for what it's worth -
how all of me is engaged?
hope and faith inflamed-
injurious and inglorious.
a cross to take on the cruise to live
the bloody anathemas that before me were proclaimed...

I was exploring conquered lands
left unconquered and unchampioned-
lands that had potential to be everything
but it was never harvested to be...

an island, isolated left devoid
of its legacy after being underseiged
I was travelling on Resurrection's road trip
serenaded by Hope's playlist

when Life provided commercials in the form of humbling skips.
bumped and bruised- from a road I didn't choose
face to face with humble pie and the diet of nothing left to lose
quintessential anorexia
starving for the option to choose so this feeling is new
and I know not what next to do...

ACCIPERE TEMPUS

take the time and breathe for thee
inhale as deeply as you need.
take the time to feel
and the moments you desire to be,
feel the fullness of yourself
and embrace its entirety... entirely.

take the time and believe in thee
for real this time,
then manifest the possibilities
you'd disappear into
and convert escapist fantasies into enjoyable realities.

take the time to see for thee
how far you've come after losing your way,
after being overwhelmed then left for dead
and see how you arrived on time for destiny with no delay.
open your eyes and see
how fear shrouded your blessings in mystery
and how you overcame such a traumatic history.

take the time you need
take the time to see
take the time to be
take the time to feel
take the time to heal
take the time to replenish
take the time to be whole
take YOUR time.

Audit of the Being

this is a time to retreat and revalue the premises we've forsaken
this is the audit of the being
where the quintessentialities are being tried in the fires of truth a
s it sears the sarcophagus of pride.
it is a dialogue of discomfort and unease,
it unmasks the frraudulencies
that have become customary in the grooves of your being.

These conversations are not for the weak
but they're frightening for the bold
they leave no room for growth if the facts are never told.
these seek the highest truths with Life's proof,
and this is a time where we earnestly introspect
what we have allowed to take root.
so they scour every which and every how
while compelling guardian angels to take a break and sit down.
this is a time to journal the internal
a time to assess the checks and balances
from experienced circumstances that we've undertaken-

these conversations, travel the deep that we deny,
they bully the lies our conscious hides
and awaken the traumas laying dormant -
uncovering the burial grounds of living things
we never thought important.
they force us to come to terms with the reality we've ignored,
after suffocating from the living fantasies we abhor.
know your truth and your being will love you more-
embrace it, embody it and it will empower you-
the you you've mistakenly,
underappreciated, mistreated and undervalued...

seek the truth
know the truth
speak the truth
be the truth

but still be kind to you.

Non Nomen 001

this is a canyon of impossibles
abstaining from one another
as though leperous and judgmental
proverbially oil and water
impossible piled on one another
jostling for all that exists not
the desire to overwhelm underwhelms
the captain steering madness better than he does the helm.
this canyon, a gumbo of "never to bes" -
hosting vision board parties
where possible abstinence is their mantra.

they sing loudly praying to Contra, riot, please-
masking their ineptitudes and penchant for being contrarieties -
the bickering of luminary beauties -
screaming Pleiades discussing the polarities and vagaries-
vying vivaciously with vigour and verve to be other-
apart from rather than a part of.
Opposites attracting and maintaining their stances.
Bad dancers in arms, opps in the heart,
colloguing on beat waning into obsolete.

this canyon filled with frivolous biddies,
rivals posing en garde,
ready to battle on their fences of doubts doing
galactic pliés and cosmic pirouettes with unseen immaculacies.
ebb and flow outdoing each other with imposter syndrome,
pretending to be the other character g
the deficiencies in their artilleries
in this canyon where these two are eternally at odds
impeding the others free will as they will on whim -
tit for tat in their pettiverse- curating karma schizophrenising Moirai -
confusion conflicts as syncretism collides-
taking each blow in stride a calamitous ride with signals fried.
these inseparables bound by putrid indignation,
stirring damnation to its most dastard degradation.

eternally these two claw and chew tooth and nail
over all things magnanimous and minuscule 'til the end of time.
a war tied during wartime with no stalemate in sight.
I echo in grief for the mediator can't sue for peace
nor is gifted reprieve to breathe or be.
so I try looking for a reason to find beauty outside
because I can no longer sit idly between sides harvesting pride-
I can no longer sit in silence witnessing and experiencing
violence between these two manufacturing rue- what am I to do,
show me a sign or point me to where I can find a reason
to unite the my heart and my mind.

ABBYSMALA

come spend your time with me
I can be so good to you
believe me- I'm so good for you!
come and spend eternity with me on Throe's soil
and make love to me in all this turmoil,
let me fill your soul with the misery only true love can dole.
spend your infinities with me
and I'll tell you the backstory
and wagers behind all your adversities;
I can show you the meticulous details in the charades-
how grief fully ordained in disarray rain dances on your parade.
I get off on your tears and tragedy
to see you suffer and struggle
makes me uncontrollably giddy and I smile happily!

come and let me bring your spirit rest!
I'd love to be the repetitive calamity behind your beating chest,
id love to be the perplexities of your vexation
and the pulse of your tribulation,
I desire for you to be so pieceful
that Planck's length is a 100 yards of unrecoverable fatalities.

come and breathe in perpetuity
that I may season it with labour
you know my twin brother but make room for me
I am she that makes saints question why
then teeming with worthlessness and genius
offer their subsistence as a measly sacrifice
only for their lord to question why?
I taught Lorelei how to lure and lie,
I took in the hell hounds and gave them purpose
all the drudgeries I breathe is in retaliation for Eve.
I made the apex of bovarism the abysmal depths of despair
I allowed the tribal fear dance of the Doldrumedans
to cast forlorn in the air

truly, I desire the zenith of despondence and dejection
I want it all for you because you intrigue and interest me
make morbid love to me in the alleys of Catatonia
under the Red Moon feeling the percussion of rue
while Malaise plays gloomy tunes of the cool blue funk....
come back to me and spend what little, little you have left
come back to me before I send...
you know who, because you wouldn't want to get sent.
so please my love, come unto me.

these tears - fall in interrupted haikus
oh, glimmer of drudgery
I pray this harvest of misery will end soon
and it ramps back up
pestilence playing poker calling the bluff of bad luck
A worst estate, with an even more maniacal fate
These tears fall and I am too insignificant to deny their impact
chaos getting its adversities intact- in fact
they fall like drops of water comets from Niagara -
metaphysical comets cometh - comma after comma-
this run on sentence of anguish persists and no one can resist-
these watery fists that hits and ne'er miss
and no prayer answered is divine enough to cease or desist
this is the onslaught of onslaughts- the big kahuna-
hardship and peril commune at their tribunal
standing firm on their verdict
any motion to appeal is met with swift refusal.
I'm down under – encapsulated in my tears
this watery submarine blocks everything but my fears
sinking to the deep- it's getting harder to breathe
and from the corner of my eye what do I see
the daunting imagery of
a macroudiae disco dancing to fast paced heart beats
panicking and, in a frenzy,-
on the outside my friends see the discord and disarray
mourn with spiked fascination and dismay
it falls down
the utopia of hope and childhood dreams
at the seams off the reams
I scream, chilling sounds never sounded so serene
Inward I retreat and these tears push forward like black Friday sales
defence frail, fortune snails and hope pales...
I miss the boy in me I who let drown for sake of my pains buoyancy
The boy I don't see, the boy I held hostage
to impress the loved ones that left me to die in irrelevancy
I do not like it here nor these tears
oh the drudgery when they can go and I can't leave...

Iunior Mihi Cara Sui

We are still playing hide and seek it seems
with the trauma you experienced as a child.
I'll still searching for the clues of rue that damaged our worldview.
I went so far from you and from the plans we had, I let you down-
I let... us down and it pains me that I abandoned you
in search of new leaving you to deal
with all the hurt I was too broken to feel.
So I heaped every bit of what I couldn't handle
on top of the poor little child I no longer knew.
I deposited the angst and anxieties,
the failures and disappointments on you-
ignoring the cries for help- playing blind to your needs
has me now weeping uncontrollably on my knees.
Had I known that this would catch up to me
I'd have made better decisions
in how I not only treated you but how I thought of you.

I buried you in anguish and still expected you
to do the work we were never taught to do.
I am so sorry for bombarding and abandoning you
while being me that still depended on you for us. I never showed you love,
I never showed you care. Loyalty wasn't meant for the easy times
and I wasn't there to be found when it hasn't been easy for you;
I paraded during your torture as though we were separate entities-
as though id retired you once I became a teenager,
a twenty year old and then entered my thirties.
I didn't know any better, couldn't have known better
and that's still not an excuse...

I robbed us of a future where we wouldn't be so maligned
by the ignorance of youth retreating from anguish and affliction-
searching for the voice of my childhood while ashamedly lost and walking
as a prisoner in divine circles seeking the pieces to the puzzle I missed the last go
round.
I robbed us of us by being me, I robbed us of strength by being weak,
I robbed us of more futures by not being present
and remaining anchored in the past.

I robbed us of the purity of your heart,
your brilliance and your growth.
I robbed us of us and the greatest and highest potency
we could have ever had.
I was scared and you were suffering,
I ran away and you were stuck
having to weigh the balance
of the cowardice I kept tithing to you.

I'm so sorry-

I've returned for what it's worth
to revive the value of our usness and to do the work
of giving you everything I took from you
that you drastically needed-
the space and time to be and to breathe,
room to play and make mistakes-
space to take up and horizons to broaden,
territory to harvest illimitably and quintessentially.

Reasons for hope, decisions of love and beauty of life.
I'm here with you, willing to earn every nanosecond
of time spent in hopes that the weight of all I've learnt
will hold ten times as much weight as the times I left.
I'm here for you little one, specifically the you in me.
I don't know it all, but we can find out together.
No parts of me left hurt or behind in isolation.
My desire is for us to be whole in the entirety of our being
and while I know I'm late-
this for me for us is the new mandate
in which we'll forever partake.
I'm sorry, for all of it-
I'm sorry still. In tears still.
Regretting it still. I'm sorry.

Little One to me: you had to move on without me, had you not...
we would've died... together. Thank you for being braver than I was...
now let's love each other better than we ever could've imagined.

GLIMMER OF DRUDGERY 02

apologies paint my padded room with bandaids for the soul-
wrapped in discomfort even the child in me cant console
so I rock myself into the annals of antiquity
recalling ptsd 'til my body becomes jittery and my spirit is fidgety.
I recall and they answer boldly as though been there quietly all along
humming macabrimonius songs
the trauma of my yesteryears holding hands
doing their best soul pain dance
every chance they get to prove I don't belong.

these apologies wait outside the edifice of sincerity
while insensitive showcases its dexterity and impiety-
Shaolin monk mastering sobriety-
a drunken mess sipping greedily ad hoc speedily
to prevent clarity on any level-
then they revel 'til the pandemonium settles-
the cooling of the kettle -
dregs rising proving the worthless mettle.

didn't we already apologise
why is there still a march to pulverise....
I still don't like it here nor does the hope inside....
its glimmer subsides and misery decides
this is where it chooses to reside
remodelling every happy memory in sight
sees recovery and smiles -
twiddles its fingers before going in its bag of tricks- it quips
"don't these bandaids itch- seems like they fail to fix-
as they pretend to trip and rip to smithereens
the peace treaty in me declared in the fiat verbalised in apologies.....
I'm sorry I failed you again- my friend-
I do not have the words to say how much I repudiate.....
maybe we can renegotiate...

Non Nomen 006

I am greater
than the initial idea of greatness
I settled for...
I am more powerful
than the initial power
I allowed to subdue me...
I am special
I am a blessing blessing...
I am abundance
wrapped in goodness...
I am perpetual harvest...

I am healing from
all traumas, grudges
ill thoughts and ill will done to me
I am forgiving my own actions
that caused hurt
whether I knew or not

I am forgiving actions
done to me
whether I knew I not.
I give love freely
I give love freely
I require myself whole
I require myself whole
and you have no place

to negotiate my worth or my standards...

BAY ABYSSMO

you will not like it here...
come ye all into the soothing unsatisfactory
comforting you with torture
come ye all
and be face to face with what makes you headless
for it is I the pre-eminent of the two baseless caldrons of rue-
I am Abyssmo
the bay from which all monsters came
come and feel this concerto of agony-
accompanied by the acapella of Tragedy.
I send all- you know me well
Hell, Hades or Dudael-

I set the seasons of Misfortune and Calamity-
upon the solstice of Unfortunate and the Equinox of Malady
I populate the seas with Distress and Desolation
I paint the very air with sorrow and suffering
you know me well- the unpleasant hell
where you send foe and friend.
I harvest rue and there is no voluntary tribute
to go in place of you.
You will not like it here...

come to me..
and feel the misery of eighteen twin flames
going out at once candle blown- angst is shown
I am that bay, incommodious finds its purpose here,
fear begs to restock its supplies and I oblige, time after time.
this is my design; catastrophe and adversity vie for my affection
whichever I cane the other raises its ableness.
procuring grief and indigence
baking negligence got the sweet tooth of pessimism.
you will not like it here

come to me

come and feel despondence in all its gallantry.
bask in the golden existence that is my savagery;
I house all here and they chant my very gloom
in unison, orphaned cherubim boom
ethereal doom that ruins and consumes
woe is whoever I choose
all are mine to view and pursue to confuse and use.
welcome to the uber abyssmality that oblivion prays to
forgetfulness is an afterthought and no one thinks here.
they die to come here and re-die when they arrive
you will not like it here

come ye all
where hope is void of itself and utterly homeless- soulless
pride walks the street more proudly than pride parades
tribulation climaxes with surreal jubilation
as it hands out devastation like coupons
a free for all as disaster free-falls after answering my call -
infinite lines so nary a ring missed-
your happiness will be eclipsed then your being dismissed.
flung to the underworld of oblivions cemetery.

come ye all, come and feel-
why you will not like it here but cant escape-
feel the dread of this misery terribly.
you know me well
I am that bay, from whence all the monsters came
drown in the macabrious divinity that is all of me-
become entrenched as you're drenched in the stench
bellowing the mating call of the Depressed
in the grip of death simultaneously
your entire being in a nefarious clench-
being stressed while stretched.

come and feel the zeal of my irrepressible misery
and incontrovertible agony.
You will not like it here,
nor will you escape my boundless lair.

GLIMMER OF DRUDGERY 07

into the abyssmality and utter darkness of Dudael
nothing goes but all arrive to wait and...
we know- we know
but I begin my ascent from the restlessness
of these Hadesian depths...
crawling on all that crawl and slither
from the first trickster then every other
that evolution put the slumber-
even the first winged singing caterpillar...
still... crawling thru the most mundane
on the most mondayest of mondays
lamenting Jeremiahcal woes
on all fours before blind foes
too hell bent on who they'll send to...
since they were sent too...

exhaustion running its illimitable marathon
morphing the sprightly into morbidly fatigued
the only reason to proceed is forsaking beliefs for sake of belief
and I don't believe stubborn bull - won't quit
crawl the shawshank way through all this....
nothing left to give
'cept the right
this is the rite of life
with the right of mind
not in his
I'm crawling still
upward bound
the score of gore
horror roars
with weeping and teeth gnashing sounds
divine crescendo- upward still
upward the momentum builds

still scared and I do not like it here

walls tiled in fear
paradise trolls the air
I'm crawling still, upward still
in this cocoon raging against whirlwinds and typhoons
I tire soon while angels out of tune learn to play the bassoon

its devilectic -weirmal at its best
anxiety milking apprehension behind my chest
upward still
no time to kill
but infinity has its death sentence
put a comma there,
as the commanders here
attempt to commandeer
get Blitzen- Rudolph is impolite
I see the light- darkness chases
the moon wines and wanes
going thru its phases
upward still
I do not like it here
I'm so tired

bearing burdens that don't belong to me
but I must for I must pick either this dastardly devilish drudgery
or the ceremonial crematorials in cemeteries
I choose life- for you and me
so the gods chose me to be John the Baptist and Christ
pave the way and bear the burden of the way....
I'm tired still, upward still
highly exhausted but closer to the goal
Santa Claus crawling thru the metaphysical chimney
to bring you hope encased in dope and administered
in love and hieroglyphic hugs

upward still
the mountain of a lifetime now Jack and Jill's Hill
fear tumbling- failure mumbling
their plans crumbling

I'm here now
emerging thru all the evolving
you can make it too
it's worth it and so are you
no lies- for there lies the skin you shed for this truth
I'm crawling still
exhausted beyond all description
dragging myself
thru the remnants of necessary affliction
I prayed for one and became my saviour
and now I've arrived- ready to be revived and purified
worn out - still....
I
crawl
in that chamber

DopebaricChamber

I ascended from the depths of my evolution,
weary and exhausted yet ready to embark on this new level of dope.
I withdrew from normalcy to assess the fullness of my newness
and so I stepped away to entrench myself in the gutters of the deep
that compels me to wrestle the darkness within and externally.

Rapt in overcoming the obstacles that trigger the best of me,
and taming the arrogance to turns my nose up
to those who haven't been as fortunate to overcome
or been blessed with the guidance to evolve.
This burden of dope, to continually evolve the truth of my core person
without lording my blessings over anyone.
This responsibility of dope reminds me that I am privileged
to be gifted with extraordinary and I am to be an exemplary steward of this bless-
ing,
it compels me to be mindful of myself and that the dope translates better
when I'm great to myself firstly but more importantly to others.
This dope clears the path for me to be good to myself
and my fellow humans regardless of beliefs, preferences and life choices.

I've spent so much time collecting the dregs of the world-
the remoulding of societal norms, my fortress strength being drained
from helping and pouring into loved ones, friends and strangers.
Feeling heavy from all the interactions and emotional dumps I've allowed myself to
carry.
Dragging my tattered spirit to the rejuvenating cocoon of Dopeness
that will decompress all the information I've ingested
from lessons and the experiences that I've been fortunate to exist in.

I stepped in the Dopebaric Chamber to refuel, recalibrate, rehumanise and realise
the importance and weight of this gift
and this time I've been filled with a more pure version of ...
...this dope...
it fulfils self while being selfless.

ENTELECHENESIS

I am the sunrise of my own darkness
the miracle worker conjuring healing elixirs
brewed for the maladies of childhood trauma.
I am the super hero saving myself from my own demise,
the most sought after prize the voice of wisdom
inside counselling the anger and naiveté show

I now know that i know now-
that I am the pre-eminence of all things legendary
unswayed and unbothered by the infirmities
of celebrated tragedies... that was me.
no longer the hypochondriac unicorn ailing in a zoo of mules
wailing about the burdens I wasn't supposed to bear
the albatross hugs that adorned me everywhere
I am stronger by what seemed like mistakes
once disheartened by the relapse and retakes

I am no longer the christ of the circle
crucifying myself for the betterment of detriment
no longer the merciful and quiet being
whose being taken for granted or taken for the fool
no longer do i wait hand and foot
for the hands and feet of them
which showcase the nothingness in me

I am no longer the insecure, unsure
doubtful and negatively self-speaking
universe crumbling within itself
I've sent it to the black hole of oblivion to be chastised then baptised
them sentenced to be Qhubified then brought to life anew
therefore I am the standard for which all dope is defined
I am the standard for which all legendary aligns
I am the pre-eminence of amazing
the greatest believer of myself
and the greatest achiever I ever met
I decree and I declare that I in all my dopeness will be
loved regarded appreciated and revered
by all but more so by me

It is with great pleasure

That I announce the name of my next pilgrimm (anything I write)

Which I began writing in 2016 its name

HBM - ARU

The Heartbreak Masterpiece: A Razed Utopia

Thank you for your love, support and patience.

dlaiaw
laluq
lilaaf

Made in the USA
Coppell, TX
08 August 2021